DASAVATAR STORIES

CEO'S

Business Technology

Optimization

DEDICATED TO MY TEACHERS AND GURU

Table of Contents

Foreword

From the stone ages, the human society has grown into the metal ages by the discovery, efficient use of metals and minerals, thereby increasing the throughput of human labor. Then came the Industrial revolution, where we accelerated the throughput of manufacturing by means of effective automation. This was followed by the Information revolution, which in its five decades has brought automation of not only engineering processes, but also service processes. Though simply termed as office automation, it has deeper penetration in manufacturing and other realms. The latest revolution of internet and mobile has taken a greater leap into throughput maximization. Thanks to the phenomena, we are now set for complete digital operation transformation. Once the society is geared and structured to operate cashless, moneyless and fearless, existence will expand to a larger platform called The Universe, over and above the current Earth based living. In the transition through the different ages, there has always been one fundamental key, and that is a shift in the factors of production.

The author has noted that any of the shifts have extensive feedback and observations, which would aid the society to move forward in this continuous journey. The author has been following the electronic data processing trend from its inception in the early seventies, to its growth in to the current information engineering and science. In today's connected society by wireless, web and social networks, information technology has become the core factor of production. It is inseparable and an integral part of business technology for any business on this earth. Fundamental education on this factor, available from the past five decades will provide a significant feedback loop. CEO is the core avatar of all corporations today that are delivering goods and services of any kind. The days have changed from those of a CEO being just aware of information technology to a CEO understanding its play and leverage. This education is acquired by means of magazines, interactions with manufacturers, institutions, analysts and CIO's. After about a couple of trillions of dollars of investment to handle this factor of production, 99% being the past failure rate, today a CEO has grown to a state of delivering results to stake holders at a much higher success rate; hovering around 40%. This by itself has given significant gains. Now a CEO has to accelerate this success rate to 98% and he/she has a choice of achieving this as we are trailblazing into the concept of Digital Society with Digitized operations. In this white space this book will be handy and provide guide lights, by showcasing situations handled by his/her predecessors in the past few decades. A CEO of today would like to infer from these stories and ignite his/her own flow on the path to delivering phenomenal results.

The author has conceived most significant and relevant situations under which CEO's of today are operating and would operate. The author has created 10 incarnations of CEO's called the Dasavatars; "Dash" standing for ten in the historic Sanskrit language, that would fit into the current organizational and business challenges. The author has outlined the background leading to the need for the avatars, and created these ten CEO's to handle the situations of business technology optimization. The author has created these heroes based on his real-life experience of dealing with successful CEO's who have leveraged the business. The CEO's of next two decades have vital inputs from this book as they are ordained with a greater challenge of increasing the productivity and reliability of Information Technology by double, at half the rate of investment. Again, a CEO is not born but evolved and groomed from a business leader level. Hence this book is vital for business leaders aspiring to become CEO's. Irrespective of whether an organization is a startup, lean, local, global...these Dasavatars will be relevant and pertinent. Knowing your customer's challenges to deliver the requirements, warrants every individual in the field of business technology to understand the mindsets of CEO's. Hence the Dasavatars also become more relevant to them.

Emerging from a punch card era to the era of IOT, the author has pooled his observations of CEO's, four decades of interactions with C level, including his own experience as Business leader, various C level positions held by him in global environments across industries into creating these Dasavatars for Business Technology Optimization. For this reason, he has selected the title CEO's BTO to enlighten this exuberant journey.

This book has the chance to be a CEO style kit built through analyzing leaders, organizations built by investment bankers, PE providers, venture capitalists and management consultants.

As business leaders and CEO's emerge with support from the academia, the author strongly believes that this book will be a handy and fundamental tool for graduates and faculties from Information Technology, Business Administration and Business Technology domains at various Universities and Research Institutions.

Author wishes all readers a great success in handling the factor of production business technology in an optimized way.

Introduction

Chief Executive Officer popularly called as CEO is the Avatar of a few centuries, who is expected to juggle the factors of production and deliver a throughput as desired by the stake holders in the gallery and their Board, setting boundaries and demanding year on year improvements from the past. Today the CEO is expected to produce quarter on quarter improvements consistently meeting to the requirements of a wide range of active and passive stakeholders including regulators, non-governmental agencies etc. CEO is supported and surrounded by a team which he is expected to enable, empower and embank to perform at their best at all times. Today's CEO's remuneration, risks and challenges are all phenomenal. For achieving the results without failing, CEO uses factors of productions such as People, Platform and Technology. Pre-Industrialization, significant factor of production was Labor, However Post-Industrialization machines have been added to the equation, yielding accelerated delivery and volumes, while the platform happened to be still manual and localized information. Information age has added IT, a higher factor of production which has increased the throughput of the man machine information combination. IT has effectively permeated all spectrums of business like planning, research & development, product development, engineering, manufacturing, materials, marketing, sales, human resources, finance and stake holder management. Thereby it has attained the name of **Business Technology** and is the prime handle and breather for a CEO at all times. The case of 2 CEO's is interesting to note in this context. One of them operating in the late years of past decade decided to reach out to all the population of the globe using Information Technology as a core technology. Another CEO believed the traditional Brick and Mortar model to help gain mind share and market share. The CEO with business technology as a core and anchor resource, expanded the reach with automated channels and reached a higher customer base across wider strata. It was deeper reach, crossing barriers of culture, language, entry exit regulations. The one with

Industrial age mindset had very limited reach. Thus, BT(IT+++) is the Critical Success Factor for the CEO of today. At the same time BT requires significant investment and caused failures in creating business advantage due to delays, cost overrun and technology obsolescence including software project failures. It is a double-edged weapon and hence CEO requires to juggle it swiftly without hurting oneself and the organization.

Hence, A CEO needs to appreciate information technology (**TAPS**CSFMS) for harnessing successful technology consistently to provide successful customer service, financial management, compliance and sustenance. **TAPS**CSFMS encompasses

- Technology adoption paths (choice of routes)
- Success and failures of the past
- Choice selection appropriate to one's Business environment
- Set technology leadership and sustain over decades
- Fine tune and modernize the technology assets
- Monetize the technology where appropriate
- Sunset irrelevant technology

TAPS is the first step and next set of sessions will cover the nuances. CSFMS is the next step and later parts of the book will cover details on the same. The fundamental for achieving success in CSFMS will be ensured by means of a thorough grounding with relevant and significant examples in **TAPS.**

Business Technology Landscape

TAPS

Business Technology Sense

In the past six decades Information Technology evolved from green screen to Web 3.0 on the cloud. The adoption of technology began from academics to commercial to social uses. Research and *incentive for research* was a driver in evolving information technology with the aid of communication technology, innovation and inventions. While grants for research like Digital corporation by ARDC [American Research and Development Corporation], funded the initiatives in the research front for converting lab technology to live technology, Venture Capitalist and PE helped investing in high threshold acceleration. This resulted in high takeoff velocity at the right stage as witnessed during the Dot Com burst that resulted in robust web and mobility, which forms an integral part of everyday life on earth today. The latest offshoot of this phenomena and rapidly growing has been cloud computing.

The Industry has adopted the technology to its benefits in gradual steps. Starting as R&D in some areas, tax incentives in some other areas, differentiator in few cases and also as a harbinger of prosperity. According to analysts such as Gartner there is a Hype Cycle for adoption and the Industrial Units are classified as Leaders, Followers and Laggard. Manufacturing Industries began the initiative to augment the manufacturing supply chain, production planning and financial accounting. Service Industries used this as an opportunity to provide differentiation and faster time to market. Government sector used this technology for governance, storage of information. While the routes are many, the reality is today we are in a situation of IT being one of the fundamental needs of society for sustenance.

Countries have adopted the technology based on their readiness to invest and capacity to experiment and venture. Countries also fall into the categories of leader, follower and laggards. While the western continents of the globe were early birds in investing and adopting, the eastern counterparts were laggards in implementing, however once on board they built capacities to lead and deliver software technology. The first 50 years belonged to the West. Then there was a shift to the East. The next 30 years will be led by the so-called BRIC countries. In essence the technology adoption is well balanced. The early adopters have a legacy to deal with in this fast-changing field with paradigm shifts, whereas the laggards have the advantage of adopting latest without much transition cost. Considering the trends, leaders of the past century require a transformation agenda to play catch-up.

People across the globe have different speed and approach to adoption. But with the dawn of internet and web, supported amply by telecom, it has been easily possible for the universal citizens to adopt early and realize benefit at will. I am remembering the days where we spent significant efforts to connect the computing machines, and later days wherein we struggled with the machine to machine wireless blue tooth technology, Symbian o/s. leading the evolution at that time. Today they are a past dream and children born after 2010 would only have a chance to see them in the Museum. In spite of the state of literacy proliferation one thing that has superseded all development is adoption to web and mobile technology. People from all walks of life and in all continents, have adopted significantly to this FLOW.

Businesses - local, state, national, continental and global have adopted information technology at different speeds and intensities. From large organizations, the adoption caught the SME segment in the last century, all the way from America to China. Electronic Data Processing (EDP) was the buzz word of leading economies in the globe in the early part, moving towards legacy systems with mainframe, mini, and networked standalones. Today parallel computing and super computers are existing realities across all continents. Businesses have adopted from EDP to OLTP to real time web. However, the businesses are yet to capitalize the real benefits of supercomputing. Research and governmental organizations have moved faster into this realm. From the purpose of automating administrative work, technology has far grown to improve many aspects and factors of production. Today core manufacturing uses IT for optimizing throughput and has moved to higher level of robotics eliminating hazardous aspects of past manufacturing techniques. Manufacturing support systems use IT for automating many of the functions with reasonable integration. Yet the islands of core manufacturing and other systems are quite disconnected. Adopting IT was the privilege of the rich companies in the beginning, however IT adoption is part of the basic DNA of any organization today. Services business evolved and grew embedding IT as core competency along with other domains, while manufacturing used IT as a critical success factor. The distribution and other middle layers adopted IT as an intermediate required state. New Businesses today are designed around IT for providing the basic USPs. The society has spent more than Ten trillion dollars in the last 50 years to reach this stage. This is equivalent of the GDP of one or two Large Nations or 15% of GDP of the globe, just to give a picture of the investment magnitude.

Core of Information Technology

The core of information technology lies in the fact that anything and everything gets converted to digits 0 and 1 and the interplay of 0 and 1 in combinations can represent events, objects etc. The technology built evolved around handling the binary code in an automated way starting with mechanical means to electronic means. Data Science evolved rapidly and was instrumental for graduation to the current information age. At present this science has matured and is trying to shift to the next layer of intelligence, taking baby steps towards Knowledge Science and Wisdom Technology. Core of information Technology can possibly be explained as

1) Visualizing everything as data and codifying same as required
2) Data conceived as 0 and 1 for handling
3) A Technology, that can handle digits with the resultant throughput being put to multitudes of use in different walks of life.
4) Today Data includes images; static and streaming and anything that can be described as content; real and virtual.

After Half a century, this technology has become common use technology and adopted by most.

In simple terms Information technology, may be understood as "Digitizing all content, Store, Transport and Use for multitudes of purpose". These were achieved by means of data stores and transported for use through programming. Like anyone on earth, this technology is basically about capturing content as our senses do, store them as in our brain and nerve systems and use appropriately with consciousness and even in unconscious states. Core focus of any business is to deliver a goods or service or value to any of the living beings. Essentially Business Technology is such a core focus and today's name for the same is Information Technology(IT). The moment in future when Artificial Intelligence will be commoditized and bundled, this offering will be changed to intelligent information technology(IIT). This in turn may graduate to knowledge technology(KT) and to end as Wisdom Technologies(WT) to ultimately turn into Life technology(LT).

In this book author is specific to handle the issues of using information technology as it is today, and for the next three to four decades as IT sets upon its transition route to IIT. Essential read for current generation of Business leaders who are at different levels of evolution of IT. For this purpose, evolution path is explained as below:

From a pure play, unstructured situation based programming in house for meeting a business need, today the field has expanded to a large arena with models for measuring capability and maturity level of organizations harnessing the technology. It has become a branch of management science like marketing, production and finance, with its own taxonomy and economy. From mere spend of less than 1% previously, today organizations spend 3-10% on this technology. With the online business gaining significant share, IT may become THE key factor of production. IT has hardware and software as two big streams. The hardware branch is more comprehensible and is aligned with known engineering principles and manufacturing norms. Hence the benefits of industrialization and manufacturing engineering research have been harnessed and net-net is predictable with reasonable creativity. The communication technology which is the connecting rod of hardware and software has also fallen in line with manufacturing principles and follows the reliability path. e.g. it is guaranteed this computer will work for x hours under these conditions with 3 Sigma uptimes accuracy. Communication networks also ensure the same. However, **SOFTWARE** is yet becoming an engineering. **SOFTWARE** is like the creative content of the movie industry, reliability of which is a chance factor. **SOFTWARE can be classified by Operating System, Application Software (COTS or custom built) and Security Software**. Over the decades' software has adopted methodologies and processes akin to other manufacturing to address the scaling and reliability issues. The result is that about 30% of software projects for custom built applications delivered has a reliability of rolling out to production. In the case of operating systems, the reliability is improving and no more we hear the common language and fear of **CRASH**. Security software is in the early stage like application software. The bottleneck for above state is requirement management. It has not become a full-fledged science leave alone becoming an engineering facet. This means the famous **GIGO** is a highly relevant factor even after 6 decades and there is no visibility that a reliable process is emerging. The promise of **WYSIWYG** (what you see is what you get) has not become a reliable phenomenon to the level as other technologies have become. A sea of change is happening with the proliferation of internet and mobile computing. The programming community is able to provide a solution that will run with certainty on a specific mobile device or through internet anywhere. The newer methods of development like Agile methodology has reduced the GIGO effect but not eliminated or removed the same. At the same time vulnerability of the solution to hacking or other security threats has reached a higher plane and volume. The technology has produced large volumes of data, stored information, hidden intelligence and buried wisdom and this dimension today is being called the Big Data. Some breakthrough is happening in pattern analysis and other domains to provide the intelligence, yet the technology has limited maturity to yield wisdom. As a result, today we are in a virtual and vulnerable situation requiring a **IT agile CEO, Business agile CIO's** and **Business Tech savvy CRO's and CFO's**.

The creation and the rise of CIO community

This community has evolved from Data processing manager to its current state. Today CIO is a key role for any organization irrespective of whether it is public or private, government or commercial, profit or nonprofit, manufacturing or service, and work or leisure. Having started at the middle management tier earlier, today things have changed and CIO is part of the top management tier of any organization. At times, in the finer corporate layers this role gets rolled into COO or CFO, especially when the entity concerned is viewing IT as being cost or operation oriented. This phenomenon could be observed frequently in Laggard organizations. However, Leader organizations accommodate CIO in the office of CEO or as part of CEO. In the Follower organizations, this is dovetailed between the states mentioned above and most possibly the role is attached to a business function. In the emerging scenario, global or multi divisional organizations have multiple CIO's for specific region/division/business. Corporate IT CIO would be an apex role deciding policies, frameworks, and standards, taking the role of a guardian of knowledge assets. At times the CIO role is bifurcated into CTO and CIO where CTO is responsible for the technology and CIO is responsible for the information sustained by the technology. This is a frequently observed phenomenon in Information Technology and Software services Industry. Due to the significant importance of information assets to business throughput, uniqueness, growth and sustainability, many business leaders run through a stint of managing information assets as a CIO prior to becoming a CEO. Considering the fact that information has become the fundamental driver of life, today more CEO's are significantly hands-on in realizing the potential of Information Technology. They consider the company of CIO as extremely vital for their growth. Hence CIO's are in great demand. We conclude by saying that a CIO is an important moving asset for any CEO.

Success and Failure to learn from

Text books cover the Information Technology evolution, adoption, and research articles. Analyst reports cover current state and future directions. CEO and CIO magazines cover combination of above in detail and variety. Software Engineering Institutes are collecting success and failure data of assessed organization, while tech and business magazines cover at random intervals, the failures, write-offs and roll back of projects. Some of the known figures are 98% failure rate two decades back, 30% success rate in the current decades. Stories to learn also include the much-hyped fear of Y2K, Dot Com burst. The manufacturers of technology also update the community with their independent journals. Marketing collaterals educate share successes stories. Research groups, customer reviews, conference papers and forums talk in detail about recent failures, challenges faced etc. In this book, the author wishes to bring focus on significant stories that are handy and relevant to CEO's at early stage, those that are matured and those that are involved in transforming companies in size, scale and operations. Also, the stories span around decades which were on different technology evolution paths and adoption space of the Gartner Curve. The wisdom they provide is phenomenal and is relevant to emerging and current technology practices.

Ten FAQs of CEO on Business Technology

IF a CEO is given a chance to raise queries possibly the following FAQ will emerge.

1.0 I have a well-established business technology available to me and my IT for more than 3 decades (with CMM level 3 capability maturity of my software development). I am Ok with the deployment and yield. What next to optimize? - *Global Industry Leader*

2.0 I am heading a business where IT is in top gear and still there is a need to integrate Business and IT. How do I embed business growth fully into my IT Systems? - **Global Business Leader**

3.0 I have a good technology for global business and I have multitude of systems and technology built on localized needs. My business technology is a forerunner in their locality. Am I OK? - **Global Technology Leader**

4.0 I am growing my business with M&A. How do I look at Business Technology Integration? - **M&A Leader**

5.0 My business technology is top order. I want to continue to be a trail blazer. How do I continue to be successful riding the technology curve? - **Technology Leader**

6.0 My business is local and am doing well in business and use of technology. I want to go global. What do I do? - **Local Industry Leader**

7.0 My business and technology are good and I am growing. How do I integrate more for growth? - **Local Business Leader**

8.0 My Business technology is not in sync with Business, and business is not growing. Can Business technology sync help me grow business? - **Leader of Stagnant Business**

9.0 I am turning around a business and how do I leverage my Business Technology to simplify the process? - **Business Turn Around Leader**

10.0 I have a good business and feel my technology is not up to the mark. How can I leverage? - **Technology Turn Around Leader**

The above set does not include questions in the minds of Industry and Business enterprises who are moving to extinction or closure

While there is no single story that will cover the specific questions, the author would like to share significant stories and indicate the linkages to the various leaders. For this purpose, the CEO's are organized as below:

GIL, GBL, GTL, MAL, TL, LIL, LBL, SBL, BTAL, TTAL
It may appear the stories have a common message for all the players, that's how the author weaves the link through the 10 CEO situations.

Business Technology Value Realization

CSFMS

Choices and selection appropriate to one's Business environment

It may sound ridiculous and naive, but we cannot escape from the obvious.

For the business leader, the purpose of his business is core. Any information technology that can aid him build, expand and sustain his business in the current and future landscapes at an affordable cost, consistently and continuously is a relevant technology.

Today plenty of choices are available in Technology Platforms, Technology Development Methodologies, and Roll Out Approaches. In fact, a Businesses leader can choose from trail blazing technologies, adopted technologies, and proven technologies. Global Analyst firms in fact offer continuous information on technology adoption curves and trends in the past two decades. This indicates that the business leader has a choice to use this info as a factor of production which can be fine-tuned to the needs of their business.

Let us list some of these:

Application Technology Platforms	Main frame, Client Server, Web...
Data Base Technology	Flat, Hierarchical, Relational DB, Columnar DB ...
Data Storage Methodology	Onsite, offsite, near-shore, off-shore, cloud, DNA...
Programming languages	3GL, 4GL...
Communication Technologies	LAN, WAN, VPN... (Wired and Wireless)

Application Development	Procure off the shelf, develop own or a combination or Software as a service(SaaS)
Development Model	In-house, Outsource or a mix
Place of development	Onsite, offsite, offshore...
Roll out approaches	Big bang, Modular
Development methodology	Water fall, Spiral, Agile...
Disaster Recovery	Near Site, Offsite, Continental including warm and hot

While this is not complete and full, one could notice that there are more than a dozen areas with multiple choices under each area. This shows that a high number of permutations / combinations exist.

Stage of Business

First and foremost criterion for the CEO is to decide the stage of his/her business say:

> Brand new start up with aspirations to become a global player with clean slate
> or
> Start up with aspiration of leadership in local operations with clean slate
> or
> Expanding in other territories with existing systems
> or
> Expanding with global foot prints with corporate tech policy
> or
> Matured stage with Technology Vision
> or
> Inflection point
> or

Turn Around situations

Role of Technology

Whether Technology is a Business supporter, Enabler or Business Driver

Financial Capacity and Budgets

Threshold for risk taking

Social and organizational acceptance of technology

Regulations and governance requirements

CEO's confidence to handle Technology

Technology Landscape of Competition

Set technology leadership and sustain over decades

It is not a must that every company and CEO needs to attempt to be at the leading edge and cutting edge of technology at all times. Each business views technology as a lever for operation, market advantage, penetration, differentiation, consolidation...depending on its technology philosophy coupled with business philosophy. For instance, in a market which is significantly not automated and operating with ledgers, printed vouchers, purchase orders and invoices (hand written or type written), with transactions done face to face across counters, an established player may continue to run the same way and sustain same level of margins. However, when expanding geographically, reconciliation would eat away additional margins. Overall expanded operations would increase revenue and absolute profit may grow, but net profitability may take a hit. A new entrant in this segment may identify this as an opportunity to set the operation with integrated information technology. The integration solution would provide computer printouts and branch to branch online transfers, including central sourcing and stock reconciliation. The new player invests in the technology infrastructure and initial capital cost, thereby cutting down operational cost and reducing per transaction cost. In this process while his/her absolute profit may not be high, net profitability would become higher. As this is a novel idea, the new player is able to sail steadily once proven, and the customer base is able to transact in a whole new way. The established player noticing the new player's growth and competition, realizes the need for introducing next stage office automation technology beyond typewriters and hand written ledgers in his/her organization. While the new player is called a Leader, the established player may be called a Follower. Few other established players may not do anything but watch the fun. But at a later time, they would realize to double up and catch along in the journey. These players may be called Laggards. This indicates that choices are of three broad types:

1. Aggressive

2. Defensive
3. Neutral

Any organization will fall in to one of the above three types. The Business strategy may be to trail blaze, adopt, or to wait and watch. A defensive organization may set a philosophy of not becoming a guinea pig in using the new technology. It may want to observe the challenges and benefits and adopt only when the technology has been vetted for easy adoption. The critical and most important factor is that there is a need for continuously improving and moving to higher gears for sustaining the technology. The main challenge for a global corporation is that different geographies may be at different technology adoption levels, and a mix of leaders, laggards and followers, unless the global headquarters has set a Unified Technology Vision and Standard. Depending on whether one is a local CEO or global CEO, the person inherits the technology state of the location and tries to catch the race. This remains possibly true for regional and divisional set ups also. The mergers and acquisitions place additional dimensions to the above with differential Business and Technology philosophies to be merged or integrated. A CEO of a parent company which is a laggard merging with a follower or a leader may be pushed to adopt newer levels of technology. As information technology has roll out and implementation costs, challenges and timelines including cultural acceptance by the users, it may so happen that a technology leader of a large corporate may be pushed to a follower or even laggard state if the economies in which they operate does leapfrog technology upgrades.

The message is that the IT race is a marathon to be run leading, following and lagging in some laps as appropriate. It is only a handful of organizations that possibly maintain continuous leadership. Even among information technology providers, a leader of last decade may become a laggard of this decade as it takes about 5-8 years to commercialize the technology and bring it to steady state while newer and simpler innovative technology takes center stage e.g. MF, CS... and IOT. CEO of these companies again have additional challenges as they have to introduce a different technology on its own turf. E.g. Implementing SAP for accounting in MS which has dynamics.... and so on.

Fine tune and modernize technology

A technology leadership program as above would have embedded this. Yet this is a specific segment that makes or breaks a business in the past century and in the years to come. Here is an amplification attempted. As has been earlier mentioned, technology implementation rolls over a decade or two for stabilization and there is an essential need for continuous fine tuning. In simple language, it is as equal to various version adoptions in addition to handling bug fixes of the OS, Application programming, Database, Communication layers etc. The so-called revolutions and inventions in various areas have led us to continually fine tune our system by means of porting to new versions, porting to new platforms, making meaningful handshakes and communications. Significant energy, budget, and focus of CEO's through their CIO's are consumed in this zone of fine tuning. While the business benefits of fine tuning may or may not be a significant one, the CEO is left with no choice but to handle this under the principles of "going concern" for Business as Usual. This becomes a necessity, though economic analysis may indicate otherwise, calling this as possible white elephant scenario, since new throughput improvement or value addition may not exist in most situations. In medical terms one may like to call this as Garage effect. While quality processes and engineering technology has improved for automobiles in the past century except for global recalls we recently witness, the IT systems are far from such a scene. A CEO is left with choice of Cadillac to electric car to driverless car at his/her table. And the toughest part is to provide the experience of a driverless car with bullock cart equivalent archaic systems. Modernization of a fleet is a challenging assignment for Airlines and it is no less for modernizing IT systems. Many modernization projects have impacted business and cost life of CIOs. For instance, every one of us would have moved through various Windows and Mac system versions.

While this is the individual effort and pain for migrating, the dimension is large for corporate IT systems. In case of Governments it is all the more challenging than Corporate. Interesting part of this modernization happens to be like catching a fast-moving train when it has left the platform where one has to board, at a time when not many engineers available with knowledge of the faster engine, not many station masters who can signal the change, and the old engine driver still trying to cope with the new mechanisms, and an obsolete train yard inspecting the defects. While the author is not wishing to place a scary situation one cannot add value unless ground reality is stated. Hence fine tuning and modernization is the core competency required for CEO, CIO and CFO together.

Monetize the technology

The previous message on fine tuning and modernization has indicated the huge financial commitment already made by businesses in sustaining the systems and keeping it relevant. This enables a CEO to look at the System Assets from the angle of monetization. While many corporations and businesses may find it difficult, global corporations have means to capitalize by way of

Internal to the company

> i) Redistribution
> ii) Consolidation
> iii) As startup investment in new markets

Capitalize in the Markets through Own Monetization program

> i) Spinoff IT companies
> ii) JV with IT companies
> iii) White labelling with service providers for bespoke

Monetize through rights and product route in the global market

> i) IPR rights as is where is state excluding new developments get stake and hive off stake on valuation
> ii) Seed Capital for Startups through Venture arms
> iii) Mandatory adoption by JV partners

This is a specialized zone and while not many CEO's may venture into this zone, Fortune CEO's have a phenomenal opportunity and only few seem to have exercised and benefitted for reasons best known to them. This is an initiative that every CEO of Fortune companies needs to take and given the fact that it will enhance shareholder wealth, this is a subject worth to be set on the Board agenda and run by the CEO along with a board advisor who has witnessed such monetization. Author is well aware of many corporations garnering billions of dollars in this arena.

Sunset the technology

The above discussion has led us into the final point. As a CEO, I have in my experience fine-tuned, upgraded, and modernized my systems. Now I am put to a situation of Paradigm Shift, because of either business model trigger or technology revamp trigger where modernization and fine tuning cannot help. Also, I am a fast-moving train and my speed is limited to the weakest link I have (The famous Goldrat's principle). My modern systems will do better if I get rid of obsolete assets. This is a situation every CFO will support a CEO and even the Board will be excited as this is a concern with on- going growth and sustenance. Sunset of obsolete systems is the most difficult challenge faced by CEO/CFO and CIO with regard to IT Assets. The famous quote is that "there are snipers which escape culling though not useful for the changed scenario ". The common example is one of the programs and technology escaping the tech policy and framework lying in a corner. At times the number might be as high as 80% of total number of assets, that elude identification in the maze. Big Data and cloud is going to add up to this in future. Like monetization this can be a direct Board Agenda run through jointly by CEO, CFO and CRO.

Dasavatars

Dasavatars are the ten manifestations of CEO's in Business technology choice making. They address the ten FAQ's in the order mentioned before with one Story to exemplify each. The stories cover subtly the other aspects associated with the choices, while predominately they elaborate the path followed by the Purush called Avatar or in simple terms The CEO. Welcome to the World of Avatars...

Avatar 1-Donald experiment

What next to optimize? *-Global Industry Leader*

I have a well-established business technology available to me and my IT for more than 3 decades (with CMM level 3 capability maturity of my software development). I am Ok with the deployment and yield. What next to optimize? - *Global Industry Leader*

An executive of a Global Leader in Financial Industry has taken charge of the bank as Group's CEO. Mr. Donald is known as Don. He is taking charge of an Entity which is spread globally across continents with foothold in 100+ countries and appears in the top 3-4 ranks on the performance charts in all the five continents where it has presence. The Entity has set trend for technology adoption and over the last two decades moved the technology up, its current software delivery processes have been assessed to be at CMM Level 3. This entity had the fortune of withstanding the global crisis a decade back, riding on its business process embedded technology. Group CEO has multiple CEO's for different business segments and regional CIO's reporting to Group CTO with a stated Corporate Technology Policy. The policy has been reviewed by Group CRO and a Group CFO who is supported by business segment CFO's reporting to Business CEO's. In any business forum, the CIO of the entity may commonly present business advancements using technology and in any technology forums the CEO will present the value of embedding technology to business. In fact, the CEO himself has handled technology, operations, business and finance before reaching this stage in different segments of business.

The Group CEO as soon as he took charge arranged a dinner meeting and during the discussion all CEO's maintained that they will ensure to keep up the tradition of Industry leadership blended with technology. Group CEO was listening to each one attentively and with a lot of satisfaction the dinner was completed. The group CEO returned to his room after dinner and somehow he was unsettled. My experience so far indicated that I am on an industry leading system backdrop and today I hear no different message from my CEO's who are equally well versed in business and technology. With this in his mind he went to sleep. Next morning instead of going to office at the usual time (he is known for his super punctuality), he went for an extended jog and postponed couple of appointments scheduled for the day to another day. His mind wandered while he jogged. What is the purpose I am going to address in this new role? Then he stumbled upon a few children in the park trying to run a race. He noticed that instead of running on a specified track allocated for each one, the children ran in a crisscross mode and at first he thought that they did not know the rule of running on separate tracks. However, he became curious and observed more. He was surprised to find that the children randomly change track and continued the race. He forgot his jogging and got engrossed watching the race. At the end, all the children reached a spot and celebrated their successful completion. His curiosity has grown and not able to control, he reached one of the children and asked what kind of race is this? The child responded saying they are not in any race but are in a sustaining and improving game to improve their ability score by the day. He asked them why do they change track and crisscross, the child responded saying that by changing the tracks we learn the hurdle points and thresholds that we share with each other and this helps in adopting common techniques available in each run for improving the next day. CEO asked them what is the name of the game. The child responded "Wiser". Group CEO in his mid-fifties was perplexed and shrugged his shoulder. He returned home and started to his workplace. As he had postponed the appointments he had the day to himself. He scheduled an emergency luncheon meeting with his Group CFO, CRO, CTO and CAO. This is the first meeting he was having with them after taking the new responsibility. Already everybody has a quizzical look, as he has rescheduled appointments which is unnatural of him, and all the more he has a luncheon meeting without any brief on the subject for discussion.

The lunch began and the Group CEO started the meeting with a smile and a concerned look. He said that he had observed something that morning and it was unsettling him. The group became anxious as they had not shared any news or information for that day, and so why was he unsettled. Group CEO narrated the story of the "Wiser" game he witnessed that morning.

Now the group got concerned as to why was he sharing this with them? Is it going to be Rejig news...??? Group CEO has intervened and asked what everyone thinks of the game. Each one shared their views and suddenly CAO who is also responsible for Strategy and HR asked a simple question. It sounds familiar and if we make our businesses run like this would we get a different universal leadership across businesses? And CFO is quick to add that our cross-balance sheet assets may produce a higher return than consolidated balance sheet of additive model. CRO said the boys were playing colloidal risk game which may help if we follow in our business. Not a single word is uttered by CTO. The group CEO was surprised. A thought came to CTO's mind that in technology we run this game, day in and day out. Our business technologies are on native specified tracks following policy and ensuring reliability. Only significant blind spot is the absence of cross track learning and porting at the policy level. Then CTO shared his thought that Business Technology has a scope to play Wiser game. Group CEO immediately had a great relief and said Eureka. Now our priority is set. Let us make our business system technology agile and portable across Business segments and sustain leadership at not only our industry level but across industry levels.

We also look for a system asset throughput level across business segments and continually improving in such a way that we can introduce paradigm shift across all business as the technology landscape changes.

With this a smart team was formed by each business segment and anchored by a wise second line of Business technologists from every region. The team has set goals to identify and list all Business technologies in existence across business segments and geographies. To their surprise unique technology exploitation was happening across various segments, some of which were local and some of which had global adoption capability. For convenience, the technological systems were subdivided into Global systems, Regional Systems, Local Systems and Ad-hoc Systems. The team presented to the Group CEO and CFO a Program named "Optima Global Technology" with a usage code of "OGT". OGT planned to set - Global Business Technology(GBT) that would be common for all representing a common dictionary, Technology Philosophy... for all businesses

1) Global business systems(GBS*) for each business common to all geographies
2) Regional business systems(RBS*) for each business common to each geography
3) Local Business systems (LBS*) for each Business common to country
4) Ad-hoc Systems (AS*) for each Business

OGT aimed to achieve the following:
a) Common Brand experience
b) Sustaining Business technology leadership through cross industry learning, plotted through GBT
c) Reduced roll out time, cost and energy per country
d) Improved technology agility and upgradation
e) Increased efficiency and effectiveness of end user training and quick cutovers
f) Sustaining both Tech leadership and Business leadership

The 5-year program has ensured that this entity is able to roll out at 50 to 60 % of their cost, and set the tones for new business rules for the industry as a whole. In addition, the institution is able to cope with the technological challenges happening once in 5-7 years with comfort and continue to deploy appropriate and state of the art technology. The group CEO would have burnt more than twice the budget he allocated but for OGT. OGT gave scope for a big exercise to handle Ad-hoc Systems and for Sunset programs.

Avatar 2-Dorathy experiment

I am heading a business where IT is in top gear and still there is a need to integrate Business and IT. How do I embed business growth fully into my IT Systems? - **Global Business Leader**

CEO Ms. Dorothy of a global organization has a strong functional organization with a clear demarcation of verticals. Her business lines are doing well and she has a common IT division which provides IT services and technology adoption services. During many a times, she gets the feedback that her organization is doing well in pockets and regions, however there is a lack of finesse of operation compared to a CEO in the case discussed earlier. She was travelling for inauguration of a new country operation in emerging markets, and en-route she had a two-hour layover. When she was waiting in the lounge, she got a new introduction and connect with a Professor from a world-renowned university. When conversation moved beyond common topics, the professor remarked casually that while functional organizations and vertical businesses are good to operate, they do not provide the real benefits of integrated businesses. He further discussed details about how the auto industry benefitted by a paradigm shift of designing vehicles for end users rather than the traditional methodology of designing in isolation of the business. After a lively and engaging discussion with the Professor, it was time for Dorothy to board the plane. She dozed off for a bit, this being a long flight leg. She had a funny dream in which she noticed that her Business head had started designing IT, and her Technology head had started designing new business'. Her dream ended, as she woke up to the in-flight preparation announcement for landing. The inauguration went great and Dorothy was happy about it. During the inaugural dinner, she chanced upon the company of a local CEO from another organization. They got engrossed in talks about local conditions for business. During the course of the conversation, she asked him his opinion on what he considers as a unique parameter in the way he runs his operation. The Local CEO said that they were driven by a philosophy that customer and business form the fundamental of any organization. Hence all their System leaders are also Business leaders and their CTOs are trained in business first and then placed in the technology landscape. Post dinner she took time with him for a breakfast meeting next morning. She was able to get more details on embedding Business into Technology and integrating Business with Technology. She returned home satisfied with the new information she had gathered. The thought of integrating and embedding ran high in her mind. She is running an organization with a structure where four Businesses have 4 vertical leaders reporting to CEO. Respective delivery teams report to respective vertical leaders. Marketing, and a Corporate IT for Business technology headed by CIO reporting to COO, Finance reporting to CFO and Sales reporting to CSO.

She created a reorg design which aims at following changes:

Each vertical leader will have a CTO. But the CTO is by means of promoting one of the Delivery Leaders. IT Managers of CIO will be distributed to each vertical along with development capabilities. These IT Managers will later transition to business after 2 years and move under corporate IT, reporting to CTO. Managers from vertical delivery will be moved as Project Managers under CIO's. After 4 years, they will be drafted back to vertical as delivery leaders. CTO now will have a technology strategy office, policy implementation, risk management and R&D lab for appropriate technology development. CTO will also have a Manager moved under him/her from each faction - Sales, Marketing, Finance etc. to create a business embedded system for corporate, winding up to COO. While IT budgets would be distributed to businesses, CTO will get an additional budget of R&D, and budget for Technology Council. Technology Council would comprise of Vertical Business Leaders and CTO. Job of the council would be to find usable cross business assets, identification of sunset technologies, and adoption of new technologies as planned by Team of CTO, CFO, COO, CEO. Over a span of five years the company now has integrated business and technology across all verticals with Dorothy's design implementation. This has resulted in embedding the business into technology as a culture and the company has now moved forward to look at integration of methods of delivery, outsourcing delivery etc.

Avatar 3-Anne experiment

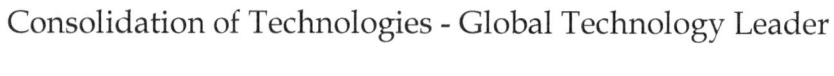

Consolidation of Technologies - Global Technology Leader

I have a good technology for global business and I have multitude of systems and technology built on localized needs. My business technology is a forerunner in their locality. Am I OK? - **Global Technology Leader**

Anne, COO of a high-ranking Corporation in the global market, got promoted to a CEO, upon retirement of the incumbent CEO. She was always impressed by the way the former CEO had run the business. The Chairman has set a very high expectation from the new CEO. The new COO is very confident that the business practices are good and very well dovetailed for respective local operations. The CTO is highly renowned in the industry and has a great fascination to be on the top of new technologies. He has leveraged the global presence and local requirements to meet the objective of providing leading and cutting edge business technologies in different countries and continents. In any technology forum, an executive of this company will always be a speaker and each of them takes great pride in their technology. New CEO is now wondering what direction she can take as all is well and settled. She was having couple of breakfast meetings with many of the leaders from technology vendor landscape. As every vendor wants to keep their company as show piece to marquee client, the meetings turned out to be good and ensured future commitment to latest technology from each vendor. In one of the meetings, a member of one vendor team called out an area of concern in integration, that quite frequently crops up in some systems. This went into the subconscious priority list of the new CEO and she got engaged into immediate operational aspects to tackle the issue at hand. One day there was a new request from Risk Committee to submit the technology risks of the corporation as a recent board member had raised a concern flag on the same. The CEO and CRO had a discussion on the same and one of the Risk managers is assigned with the project to carry out detailed analysis and study. The risk manager conducted research with the support of a crack team (comprising of people from IT, Finance, Business across the continent), and the team is surprised that the principle of local optimization has worked in various technology spheres. Global maximum spend is happening in the corporation as significant effort and big budget is spent in continuously integrating the islands. Significant learning and relearning is required for business and technology executives when transferred between continents, even when in the same business vertical. For instance, Sales executive will use technology "A" based system in continent "B", while upon transfer he/she needs to learn technology "C" based system in Continent "A". Similar to different business silos, the corporation had technology silos with business and continents interspersed making a Maze. When a business or a geography needs to be merged the major bottleneck and stumbling block is the Technology integration and capacity to negotiate better terms with vendors on a scale basis is missing, resulting in total high cost. The Risk committee has given a direction to CEO to address the risk in 12 months' time. CEO, CTO and CIOs meet on a workshop and technology teams realized that in their enthusiasm to be evangelist of specific technology, they have made the holistic landscape very messy.

It took 9 months for the CTO's team, with the help of consultants to arrive at a specific technology most suited for the business functions, and appropriate pricing models for external vendors. The globe was divided in to three zones and zone 1 embraced Technology 1, zone 2 embraced Technology 2 and zone 3 embraced Technology 3. Technology 1 is to be used for all customer facing operations. Technology 3 is to be used for all middle office and Technology 2 for all back-office operations. This will reduce complexity to 20%. This has been set as phase 1 with a time line of 2 years and a savings of 30% annually. All technology vendors have been given a Proof of Concept for narrowing down on two technologies instead of three and the value options is 12 months' time validity for a period of 5 years. The project was carried forward and the corporation achieved 20% savings, and a significant improvement of rotation of executives as learning cycle impediment is reduced. The corporation continued to be on the best of technology, but with a difference "manageable diversity" and global optimization. Post POC two technologies have been selected and third technology is sunset.

Avatar 4- Ryan experiment

Inorganic Growth Leaders Technology Choices

I am growing my business with M&A. How do I look at Business Technology Integration? - **M&A Leader**

Though limited in numbers, couple of leaders grow their organization by inorganic process and build their core competency in expanding, scaling up, spreading wings through inorganic processes of organization development. While one organization might have been grown organically further growth may happen by means of acquisitions. In such situations one may come across multiple leaders taking reins at different points of time. Mr. Ryan, CEO who is well versed in M&A joined a leading Insurance Corporation with presence across three continents, and a game plan to acquire presence in all the large continents. His team is geared to identify targets of business to be acquired in the respective local markets. The objective was to look at targets that will not only give foothold but also significant thought leadership and market share. In the target evaluation, prime objective is market share and thought leadership. Any player in any market in the financial industry would normally be a technology leader also. There will be conflicts of multiple technology perspectives, ideologies, philosophies, patronage and specialties. This poses a great challenge to the CEO of integration as every business CEO involved in the M&A have their own principles and ideas of integration.

The CEO of this organization has set up a lab at the nerve center of his organization with its own technology capabilities and capacities. To augment he has tied up an offshore which can scale up and scale down dynamically. His M&A team while doing due diligence would make it a point to conduct full technology architecture walk through and a small detail team will make in-depth analysis of the capacities, capabilities and specialties. This will be used at the lab to come up with a plan for implementation and integration. The lab does not necessarily come up with piecemeal absorption, integration and retention mode of technology. The lab needs to come up with a program of 9 months' implementation sometimes retaining whole system or even rejecting whole current technology of the target. For one acquisition, usually 10-15 targets are considered, this is an enormous load and investment. This core team, has over the years obtained the core competency to asses many options and has developed methodologies to place technologies in perspective. This team was able to plough back the learning, post implementations and has built a robust model that will maximize the objective. The situation is like mapping the few trains that are running to schedule and agendas in their respective countries to be assembled and disassembled in such a way that catastrophes are avoided and all trains run with higher speed, capacity and durability. Sometimes the cars are modernized and at times engines are changed. As the industry vertical is common, the lab has only rarely faced with the task of replacing the entire cars and engine. The lab has also developed a gearing up model using any technology relevant to the overall business.

In the final evaluation of the target, objective selection will be made while the lab would have implementation plan for any target selected. The one setback the CEO noted is that only the core team in the lab is rich in this knowhow and becomes a key to his success. The CEO identified that it may become a constraint and bottleneck in the future and has implemented a yearly review for enhancing the capabilities and scaling up the team for the future growing demands. He has created thus three to four modules of such teams. The post-merger plan kicks off and a 9 months' time window is given as sacrosanct and this team is the single face, from target study times to implementation post acquisition. Protection of IP assets of the lab is also a responsibility of this team so that pilferage do not happen during study and thereafter. Most of the occasions his teams were able to deliver on time and within reasonable budgets. The upfront investment in the lab he made helped him optimize overall investment on post-merger or acquisition technology integration.

After few years, he has noticed that he is sitting on IPs which were good and agile but dropped due to alignment with the objective. He created another organization in a jv, made to hive off the IPs creating a market of its own and monetized the value paid during M&A. However, he had a different team to do the above, as prime interest of the lab is BTO as per objective of M&A.

Inorganic growth is the way of life for specific breed of CEO's who grow, merge, demerge, and consolidate their organizations across globe and sustain leadership, change competency and relevance to the present. While business sense and purpose is achieved in this model, there is a perennial question of technology options as the constituents of a merger, demerger or consolidation provides a plethora of conflicts and compulsions from information and business technology angle.

The technology leaders of the merged companies, served with the implemented module, at times moved to research lab and on some occasions, chose to leave. However, business process assets have always remained intact giving the competitive advantage.

In a similar situation, a CEO of an asset management company created a huge project during integration with a 3 year terms of reference, however the CEO ended up taking five years. The CEO had used the traditional process of forming a task force, selecting the vendor with M&A situation delivery experience, forming global steering committee, tracking and review.

Avatar 5-Bob experiment

Sustaining Technology Leadership

My business technology is top order. I want to continue to be a trail blazer. How do I continue to be successful riding the technology curve? - **Technology Leader**

A deep observation over decades of technology adoption curve for information technology indicates that Fast track items hover around 3-5 years for adoption, while long fuse items take couple of decades for widespread adoption. CIOs and CEOs have been broadly classified as Leaders, Followers and Laggards. Technology adoption DNA of the organization is built significantly on the technology risk DNA of CEO and CIO. Once an organization is in the Leadership position invariably the trend is continued, but for Force majeure. The movement also happens in the direction, laggard to follower to leader over decades in the life cycle of organizations. Very few exceptional organizations start right at the leader position and stay put, after every tech revolution.

A CEO of a global bank rose from the ranks of the bank. He is helped by a team of CIO, CTO and CRO who are also well entrenched in creating appropriate technology at early adoption mode. For the next decade CEO has to grow and continue the DNA.

Bob, CEO of this organization head quartered in USA wanted to understand how this DNA is formed and what is the capability and maturity of organization to continue leadership. He has engaged a consortium of global consultants in the field of Technology Surveys, Industry Analysis and Bench marking. The team is given a terms of reference " Framework to keep growing our Technology Adoption as Early Adaptors". The Consultants in addition to their expertise in the diversified fields, used researches on adoption curve s and presented an Apt Technology Framework(ATF). The consultants noted the following trends:

- Business technologies tend to take couple of decades to get deep rooted and become BAU and spanning over half a century of useful life before getting retired e.g. ALPMs, ATMS, Mainframes, Database Technologies, Internet, Robotic...
- Early adaptors appear to spend more investments in the early phase, but the investments give a higher return in the subsequent phases as they are ahead of curve and are able to leap frog the market acquisition, operational effectiveness, financial excellence and organizational sustainability
- While Vision and Mission tries to include the intent, the leaders seem to have a specific business technology purpose declaration in sync with the business purpose. Leaders also inculcate Path breaking or Paradigm Changing as part of the culture
- Deep insights into progress of emerging technologies indicate that many such initiatives have sponsorship and participation in the evolution stages, from leading business' and early adaptors
- While not frequently, at times such leaders establish subsidiaries or spinoff core technology organizations to create proprietary business technologies and monetize during maturity phase

CEO and the board was presented with the Framework code named "Einstein Fifty" and basic tenets of the framework included a continuous process of design, progress and review by Board and CEO /CFO/CTO/CRO and CIO. Efficacy of the process is slated to be assessed by Consultants once in five years. The organization built technologies, adopted early, invented, monetized and retired technology assets in a regular manner with specific periodicity and sustained business technology leadership.

Avatar 6-Mark experiment

Globalization of Business

My business is local and am doing well in business and use of technology. I want to go global. What do I do? - **Local Industry Leader**

An industry leader in an emerging market with unique services in an emerging field noted that there is possibility of offering the same to global population. The leader has a gut feeling that industry leadership will be sustained at global level. The Board had a meeting with the CEO Mark, who has awareness of global scenario and mandated a globalization program. The CEO has a good friend, another expert who has rolled out global business and is retired from active business recently. They had become friends during an expedition trip. The CEO reached out to him and found that a trip to a jungle resort may be a journey to the liking of both. The CEO immediately arranged for an escapade into the wilderness... All logistics were made and the days were spent on nature treks and hikes from 8AM to 4 PM. Between 6 PM and 7 PM the two could spend quality chat time over local specialty health drinks. Post dinner a one hour sky watch and star gazing program was the daily routine. The CEO noted that the session between 6and 7 in the evening was ideal for common discussions. On the first day, he shared his requirements of going global. His friend readily shared stories of continental business rollouts experienced by him and many of his clients and on the concluding day of their trip set a program for the CEO which he was willing to review once every year.

The CEO noted that the underlining factor for globalization of service business is Business embedded with Technology of the era. The CEO called a meeting of CFO, CTO, CSO, CRO and CIO and shared his plan:

Let us grow country by country and continent by continent starting with the target continent

Let us formulate CRO, CFO guidelines for each country business

Let CTO and CIO use this guideline and formulate Technology policy for each country including Business Technology rollout models and programs

Let us budget for each country roll out and a rollout calendar including investment and return calendar

Let us present to board and obtain necessary clearances'

Let us keep in mind that we are and want to be a continuous leader in the business segment, from local to global like the xxx of the world

Our uniqueness is our core DNA and let us continue the same

Ground rule

Launch business only when we are ready to deploy the Business technology in the market

Our business technology needs to continue to top the market and win customers first and laurels eventually

The day we do marketing launch we should be able to roll out technology in parallel, and in a quarter cutover to regular scale adoption

Chief Strategy officer will anchor the program and update us of progress in each country month after month, and before launch

A country launch lead time is three quarters maximum and roll out of technology is 6 months to begin with, and 60 days after 5 countries in a continent

A Country Guide Book was the result, and business launch is timed along with completed technology roll out for markets. Technology investments upfront get accounted as startup cost

Country after country the CSO reviewed programs and Policies got appended or amended. In two decades' the business rollouts happened in multiple continents and Core Technology is the Darling to get mind share. Market share follows later as business is baked in to technology. After two to three years, bench marks have been made for future rollouts and with reduced timeline, cost line and embedded learning. After two years, a roll out steering committee is formed for future roll outs. Simultaneously a program is started for complexity reduction in global roll outs and system streamlining activities are undertaken. Business practice value engineering team is formed at headquarters for federated value gains.

Avatar 7- Susan experiment

Business Technology Integration

My business and technology are good and I am growing. How do I integrate more for growth? - **Local Business Leader**

A company in the manufacturing sector is delivering goods and post sales service for its earthmoving equipments. The CEO Susan has set good manufacturing processes and quality systems; she has an eye for business requirements and market dynamics in this concentrated customer market segment. In order to realize the benefits of using technology for business processes she has encouraged her executive team to deploy technologies for output improvement. With zeal and support the executives used the young brains in the company who have joined as Graduate Engineer Trainees for developing local systems for their functions, with speed and agility. In the meantime, she has also got an MIS team which is well recognized by the IT industry in her country and a value engineering team which brings in manufacturing automation. Now she is in the stage to expand and set foot hold in the mid-level market which is large, spread across the nation and with profit on the operation mindset. This is a very different approach and initiative, from the mining sector hitherto she was delivering and leading previously. She has consulted many experts on the move and noted that throughput enhancements and simplicity will lead to a superior delivery process and return for her operations as she aims to gain leadership in the new segment. She has engaged global engineering and process consultants requesting them to implement improvements and changes. A study by a couple of them indicated that she has a bottleneck in the form of complex integrated mainframe system with silo PC based systems, each serving a good purpose, however bearing the risk of dying moments of this technology. She attended a breakfast briefing with leaders the other day at another city and during that time, one of the participants had mentioned something about bedrock systems. She got curious and invited him to her office and engaged him to define bed rock systems, that can integrate business technology and business processes. The expert visited with a team and listed various business processes, technologies including IT, manufacturing, storage, distribution, factory and financial process automation.

It was not a surprise to him that the sophisticated integrated data management system well designed over years has become a **bottleneck** due to proprietary and "difficulty to understand by all" problems. Hence the individual process owners have resorted to easy to learn and adopt automation, varying from no data base to clipper based systems. Owing to the same factor CNC machines had their own systems and engineering department with their own scanning and image printing processes. The expert realized that for a small operation they have too many footprints and walk paths that are alien to each other, instead they should be bridging the process gaps creating islands of excellence. Expert called for a seminar attended by the CEO and her executive team and requested everyone to show case their business automation from CNC to IT to Parts picking. The executives went through the exhibition and started realizing duplicity, incompatibility and block holes created in their zeal to auto mate quickly with their own budgets and not understanding the IDMS and its usefulness to them, all this for want of urgency and one up mindset.

The expert spent time with them and set critical success factors for the Business, current and future new segments (which happen to be speed of delivery, less downtime, specialized manufacturing and local support at a cost market can pay). This resulted in the following few significant steps

- Integration of MRP, ERP, CNC, Engineering, Marketing, Sales, Warehouse and Finance systems which are through IDMS and silo other systems
- Connecting Warehouses through information satellites
- Phase out program for the IDMS with other products in the market
- Sunset program for the proprietary legacy hardware and software

- An integrated business technology development framework including stake holders from the start, and simple communication of specialized manufacturing and information technology to the executive team, and learning sessions for all the workforce

A time frame of 2-3 years was set for the program while initiatives were taken to prepare for market launch in the new segment. Instead of talking in terms of quarters for delivery, the product range has been divided into Strangers, Repeaters, Runners. Delivery period, processes and automation have also been aligned to the same. Whole company started talking about throughput instead of output as earlier and provision was still made to create quick satellite systems that were well connected to the main systems and operational manuals. The program contained quick hit projects, one-off short-term integrations and a 24-month change over project. During this period a small team comprising of integrated functionaries has been formed to create niche capacities in the new segment venture, and for the pilot projects to be carried out. At the end of four years CEO has managed to reach the leadership in all the segments and establish new business segments.

Avatar 8- Helen experiment

Technology for Revitalizing Business Growth

My Business technology is not in sync with Business, and business is not growing. Can Business technology sync help me grow business? - **Leader of Stagnant Business**

A local bank in the Western Hemisphere has well-established itself over the decades, starting journey from a small branch, to branches all over the country. This bank was known for its personalized service by a banker, who has the unique touch and feel for every customer. The bank has automated its business operations with ATMs, IT Kiosk and a well-known legacy information technology which was state of the art in the yester years. It covered the generation of 1970's and was meeting its needs and growth. The bank started stagnating from the beginning of the year 2000. The bank used multiple proven tested marketing programs and strategies for getting out of the situation and none of them clicked. At this hour, the Bank faced a calamity as its cherished leader passed away and chose an insider over an outsider to lead and bring about turn around. By a strange decision which cannot be explained convincingly, the Board has decided to make CTO Helen as CEO in place of the lost leader. This was an added shock to the market which was expecting the bank to select a turnaround artist from the market to rejuvenate growth. Stocks tumbled. Our hero is the CEO who was hitherto a CTO of the bank. She has grown to the ranks from joining as an automation executive, 25 years ago.

Helen realized that while she is glued to the business and followed the directions of the business in providing the best technology, she has a limitation of understanding the interplay of business and growth factors. As per automated surveys the customer satisfaction was ranking high in the past few decades and her bank was faring pretty well in the industry and market. She is familiar with key customers and as a first step she visited few customers who are still doing good business with the bank and had discussions. One of the customer spelt that his companies' new executive team found the bank stagnating and stifling to deal with in the past decade. She noticed a silver line in this and spent a few hours with her sales team, accounts team etc. While she noticed that the customers operational team was comfortable in dealing with the technology provided by the bank, the younger generation of the customer's employees found it cumbersome and have slowly drifted towards an emerging bank which was providing a flexible technology, which helped better transact on the go, across the country and even overseas. They all have slowly moved their retail banking needs to the emerging bank and kept proven investment banking needs with the trusted existing bank. Over a period of 5-6 years the company had shifted many folios to banks that support on the Go business as got-to providers. However, this silent and significant change has not been picked up by the bank she headed unfortunately. She now understood that connect with emerging trends and generations' requirements was missing and this resulted in no forewarning, buried under "We have best technology Syndrome" situation.

She engaged a demographic expert to study the customer profile from the angle of changing generations in their operations and analyzed the results. The baby boomers of the yester years who became solid customers with the bank when it provided Technology based solutions in the past century, when the market was providing brick and mortar banking are all on the verge of retirement. With this blind spot, bank has failed to recognize the upheaval so far. The job is cut out for the CTO turned CEO. Her core competency is to provide a technology that is appreciated by customer folks and enables them to do their jobs better. She slept over the thought and when she woke up, her CTO instinct usurped. She moved the banks business leader in the middle level who has a good view on the market trends to lead the Appropriate Technology project. The project is given 6 months' window to present a business technology that can retain current generation, next generation and future generation customers. It was a night mare for the Technology team which was nourished by the then CTO and now CEO. The Project Leader has started rolling out unrealistic requirements which is beyond their comprehension. In reality a gap emerged. The new leader was asking for things which will cost more time and money in the proven tech process of this bank. An explosive meeting was on the cards for the Leader and technology teams with CEO. In the meeting, suddenly one of the Technology team member who is in mid-forties and recently joined the team raised hands. He said I see a solution. All participants agreed to hear him out. He asked the participants to view the technology outside-in instead of current inside-out. He further questioned "Can we create new assets and bridge them to existing assets using architectural advantages along with the use of emerging business technologies?". The team is not confident but found a meaning in his approach. They worked together using existing systems, engaging experts from SOA architecture groups, embedded technology groups, Mobile technology groups and Internet technology groups. They arrived at a contour and decided to use agile method of development instead of water fall for this project. Instead of eight months the project overran till 15 months in spite of agile methodology. At the end, they were able to deliver a business technology that provided brick and mortar trust comfort, along with operational ease of not only mouse clicks but mobile phones, without compromising the robustness of the proven business rules. The pilot was rolled out in one county and it became a great success and business once again started building up. The technology was show cased in banking association conference and got extreme appreciation. Instead of sequential launching CEO went ahead with two quarter roll out, along with marketing promotion to customers' employee spectrum giving early adopter rewards and incentives. While the bottom line had a good dip in the next few quarters the bank has overcome the stagnation and bounced back to fast growth trajectory.

Avatar 9- Hogan experiment

Turning Around the Business with Business Technology as a Ply

I am turning around a business and how do I leverage my Business Technology to simplify the process? –
Business Turn Around Leader

Mr. Hogan is a well-known turnaround artiste and is based out of New York. His profession is to acquire companies which have potential but are in the red zone, turn them around in two to three years, and hive them off to new buyers for a good valuation. He is in this business for more than two decades and has 70:30 success rate of turn around. He is proud of his office on Broadway on the topmost floor of a NY high story. He likes the 360-degree view of the rivers from his room. Hogan's team that evening, presented him with a couple of new opportunities to consider. While he was glancing the list, he stood up and looked around. He was surprised to notice a vendor in the square below selling burgers without collecting cash. He was curious and went down to the square and ordered his favorite burger. The vendor gave him his burger and asked Hogan to wave the mobile in front of a monitor for payment. Risk taker Hogan did so as if it is a calling. The Vendor smiled and said that the payment went through and thanked him. Hogan shrugged and walked off wondering what revenue model is this? Once he reached his office he went through his list and picked up his next target: a retailer in another continent with multiple shops across the vast continent. The retailer was doing well and the business was in red in spite of huge transaction volumes and a brand name. Hogan planned to shift for the next few years to head this retailer as CEO and turnaround the business. Hogan worked out his economics and went ahead with the buy, after a thorough study that this company had good customer fulfillment, has turnover of stocks, reasonable cost control and yet was cash starved which he thought should be the primary focus area.

He set himself to the central store in the continent and started living there. His one quarter was spent on visiting more than 30 countries and 60 stores. Overall he noted that infrastructure is good, marketing ads are good, staff appears to know business and customer needs. However, a major surprise was the stock section which always had waiting containers and was running busy for three shifts like a beehive type model. He also noticed that Finance is also busy and active for late hours and IT headquarters was three shift operation and seeking huge maintenance budget and long list of ongoing issue resolutions in spite of best ERP.

He came back to New York to arrange for further funding for next four quarters and headed back. When he was in NY he was able to have a deep glimpse of the Chinese picture on his wall. He was feeling that though the picture seemed complicated, it draws him to focus on a flow. His mind is impressed with the smooth flow continuously catching his attention, in-spite of the complicated rules and other components of the picture. He saw glow in the direction was because of the painting mix, a marvel that resonates well with the light and guide motion. He went back to the drawing sheet and noted that this retail business has simplified and standardized many aspects of operation with a top information technology platform serving as the backbone. Yet there is no glow, no guide stock build up, profitability drainers and specifically slow moving stocks. He felt he stumbled upon the focus area. He called his IT head and showed him a copy of the picture on his NY office wall which he had captured and stored on his iPad. The IT head glided through the picture altered sizes, magnified and reduced, taking a deep look at it from all possible angles. Then she called out that the guiding that is felt, is by the intelligent use of the paint possibly and the flow happens with the natural wisdom of the viewer. Hogan and IT head split for the day.

The week went without any new action. On Friday, the IT head requested two days' full time and prime time meeting engagement off-site with Hogan and Hogan readily agreed. Hogan after a good and relaxing weekend stepped into the offsite and he was greeted by energetic IT head. During the breakfast, IT head hinted to Hogan that she would like to share her IT strategy for addressing the current needs. After breakfast, she took Hogan straight to a hall where Hogan noticed 7 large TV screens named Dynamic Infrastructure Mart, Intelligent Supply Chain, Wisdom driven Business Rules, New Age Self billing mobile stations, Integration with Suppliers Systems, Customer banker exchange and Agile Systems Development. The first TV was powered and the presentation explained flexible design mart with low value, mid value and high value sections in the standard floor space with flexible arrangements guided by a visitor demand analytical software. IT head explained that based on seasonal movements, the store can be made to look familiar but with flexibility and variety without stereotype single store format. Every customer id is recognized and based on their recent purchase they have a choice to get tour guide in their mobile. The tour guide is prepared by the team on a weekly basis. App auto download sockets will be available at welcome zone. Same software provides guidance to the loading team based on stock movement and billing. Hogan was impressed. IT head took him to next TV where an Intelligent Supply Chain SW is displayed using principles of Kanban and interconnection to supplier IT and Logistics. This integrates with the customer demand software explained earlier. The pattern analysis forms the core of this section. It orders and receives low value item lots as scheduled depending on bin consumptions and restocking, mid value items as selective ordering with periodic stocking, and high value items on Kan ban mode as the item is cleared. The next station explained a Knowledge Engine to be developed using pattern analysis intelligence and big data, and arrives at Business rules which will work under SOA mode with previous two systems. The wisdom engine has provision for wisdom accumulation and synthesis of business rules periodically. Hogan picked up his next coffee and moved around in excitement. IT head skipped the 4th TV and came to 5th and explained to Hogan the detailed plans and programs for integration with supplier systems using SOA. Quickly IT head moved to next TV and explained Customer banker Exchange, where the customers will be able to securely login to their bank systems and set limits for funds transfer to mart account and would have options to get mart credit line from other bankers too. Then IT head brought Hogan back to the 4th TV and ran the demo. The demo was that of a new age desk where customer can wave the phone for billing. This phone has pre-limits set for the session by bankers, and also instantly uses royalty rewards and offers at the time of billing. Hogan is beaming with excitement at this point. Then IT head explained the final station of his approach was to achieve the above through Agile Systems Development, SOA and integrating with existing infrastructure and technology landscape. Hogan asked IT head Helen if the same could be presented to all Business leaders of the company the next day. Hogan called his office and instructed to pull all business leaders in the continent to converge at the venue next day morning by breakfast. The next day at breakfast, Hogan declared Project Trail Blazer with theme "Pick up, Flash and Checkout". He asked everyone to hold their surprise until the end of the tour. Helen took charge and walked through the demo in detail. Post Tea the excited team had only two questions? When will this happen and Who will get early bird option. Hogan said this is a 24 months' program with first roll out in 5 marts in 6 months and then it will be quarterly roll out for rest. The lot immediately selected the first 5 marts and they announced their champion to work with. Balance quarterly lots were decided and they too nominated their champions. Hogan stepped in and formed a program group comprising of all champions from day 1 and agreed to lead the program group.

Thus, it took not 24 months but about 30 months for completion and the first few marts had a delay of 2 months. However, this has created all round excitement amongst customers and resulted in increased customer flow. Revenue increased, Profits increased and there was enhanced good will from suppliers and bankers. Then Hogan is all set for negotiating the value gains with a large European chain who wants to enter the market in multiple segments, so that he can get back to his Manhattan office.

Avatar 10-Michelle experiment

Turning Around Technology

I have a good business and feel my technology is not up to the mark. How can I leverage? - **Technology Turn Around Leader**

A global insurance company has a very good business model and is growing by verticals. The businesses built over three decades has established leadership and only during the turn of the past century was stuck with a legacy technology. While a global brand, it's channels for distribution are limited to trusted agent model. Agent commissions are garnering a great amount of margin. Each vertical has its own technology CIO who reports into Finance and Admin. The systems are silos of their own and they will not talk with other verticals. A tiny team consolidates in to F&A at group headquarters, and any cross examination or cross monetization of assets is a very challenging job. Within each vertical depending on their preference, plethora of agency systems, commission calculators and highly person centric underwriting systems had their say. CIO was the ring master of the circus pulling the combined act together. While other industries were moving to channel by channel delivery model, this group was still on a single channel of delivery. The group's Board has mandated adding newer channels like ATM, Internet and consolidated Technology. The Group CFO recruited a group CIO who is a veteran of handling multiple channels and latest technologies. The usual saying that "This works for the other industry and not for insurance" is the first hurdle group CIO has to face. Michelle the group CIO has the job to Turn around Technology.

Michelle realized that she can leverage in the following manner:

- Make the systems talk to each other
- Introduce ACORD Standards
- Create a Joint Venture offshore unit for emerging technology with a technology partner and a service provider
- Expose the CIO's and teams to a local bank which has implemented Service Oriented Architecture

Thus, she went ahead setting two non-negotiable standards announced by CEO's of respective businesses through Chairman.

A. ACORD standard adoption by all businesses in 5 years' time

B. Business to be delivered through Agency, Internet and Branch Kiosk in 3 years' time

ACORD implementation group was formed, headed by the Chairman and allotted a specific budget where all CEOs and Group CIO's are partners. Channel implementation group was formed under Chairmanship of Michelle and members were CFOs and CIOs. A new position called CTO was sanctioned with the goal to introduce SOA. Michelle lead the JV in European offshore for developing internet channel technology and a new company was created to develop next generation branch-kiosk technology integrated with mobility technology at its headquarters. One of the veterans from ATM manufacture and Tablet manufacture industry was made in charge of the Technology venture. Already the major vendors of the verticals for technology supply are leading global vendors. They have all been asked to present their proof of concept for SOA adoption and Channel integration for their respective verticals. Since many backbone systems are legacy systems with much of bespoke development, all the bespoke maintenance and enhancements teams have been advised to get certified for SEICMM Level 3. In three years time the Insurance company rolled out new channels the mobile channels being a phenomenal hit. The internet technology using ACORD standard from the European subsidiary was rolled out in Asia, Africa, Europe and America in that order. In 5 years' time the ACORD standard has been implemented across the globe and the company has become champion for ACORD implementation. Micelle has been able to turn around the IT in a non-disruptive manner. She has produced a global, regional and local model of single foundation system which has strength, reliability, sustainability, flexibility, speed and agility.

Conclusion

CEO has a choice, challenge and chance to set the right business technology for business growth, sustenance and proliferation. Billions of Dollars are spent by CEO's in choosing their business technology and it is quite common to learn from failures and successes of their choices. However, post industrial revolution, after manufacturing automation, the next big revolution is information. Information Technology had a higher failure rate to implement. Over the second half of the past century, it has stabilized to make the dream "what you see is what you get" a reality. With embedded technology, robotics, and mobility today there is no Business Technology without core information technology and they can be called as synonymous. This book has shared significant success stories distilled out of failures galore. Billion Dollar big bang failures are quite common across continents, decades after decades, and technology after technology. Numerous multi-million dollar bespoke developments ran through rough weather and went down the drain. Countless new technology initiatives did not cross POC stages. However, a CEO has no choice. Manufacturing was automated in the first industrial revolution; data is automated in the IT revolution and the next centuries will see Knowledge automation moving from digitized manual processes to digital process. For the next few decades agile may be the route till robots take over software automation. That will be the next paradigm shift a CEO/CIO combine has to handle. There is no one method to CEO's BTO. However, a CEO has reasonable and relevant choices for different phases of the journey while riding a particular business horse.

Ten avatars Don, Dorothy, Anne, Ryan, Bob, Mark, Susan, Helen, Hogan and Michelle explained in the stories above are guiding beacons like the one in the airports that provide landing aid for the flight Captain.

Reference

The stories are based on real life situations, with suggestive names and situations interchanged and integrated from many instances, to cogently cover the ten questions posed.

Dasavatar is an imagination of the author and the essence is derived from learning out of lessons, books, journals, real life, corporate presentations etc. and from real life experiments, experiences over the decades in handling business technology for CEO, by CEO and of CEO

Acknowledgements

The author acknowledges with gratitude the support provided by his life partner, family members, guru, coach and colleagues who have helped him in the journey to write and publish this book.

The author expresses deep gratitude to the corporate leaders he has come across and worked with for decades across the globe and the inspirations provided by them.

The author thanks god for the divine directions, that set a calling on him for writing this book.

END

www.ingramcontent.com/pod-product-compliance
Lightning Source LLC
Chambersburg PA
CBHW070818180526
45168CB00002B/662